HISTORY ENCYCLOPEDIA

THE FRENCH REVOLUTION

An imprint of Om Books International

Contents

Reformation	4
Counter-Reformation	5
Aristocratic Revolt in France	6
Events of 1789	8
New French Regime	10
French Reign of Terror	12
Napoleon Bonaparte	14
The Napoleonic Era	16
Industrial Revolution	18
Effects of Industrial Revolution	20
Social Impact of the Industrial Revolution	22
Introduction of Laws	23
Revolutions of 1848	24
Use of Force to Suppress Revolutions	25
Romanticism	26
Romanticism and the Writers and Poets	27
Romanticism in the Arts	28
Realism	30
Scientific Positivism	31
Logical Positivism	32

The French Revolution

1789

The French Revolution, also known as the Revolution of 1789, dramatically changed France and brought the old regime to an end. The reasons for the revolution were different from the resentment amongst the bourgeoisie, who felt excluded from the power. The antipathy continued with the peasants who wanted to change the feudal setup, and philosophers who wanted to reform the political and social scene. The other reasons included France's involvement in the American Revolution that brought about huge economical problems, which also played an important role in the revolution.

The population of France comprised 98 per cent of common people, but, they did not have any say. They wanted equal representation, so they debated over the voting process and, soon, the third estate unofficially took over the title of national assembly. When clerical deputies and liberal nobles joined them, Louis XVI took all three orders into his new assembly.

The National Assembly of 1789 was a revolutionary assembly with all its representatives from the third estate. On 14th July, they stormed into the Bastille Fortress. The hysteria brought peasants to the streets, who looted and burned the homes of tax collectors and landlords, and thereby ensured that feudalism would be abolished.

Reformation

Martin Luther

Reformation was the religious revolution that occurred during the sixteenth century, led by Martin Luther and John Calvin, among others. It had multiple effects in all spheres, from political to economic to social and became the foundation of the Protestant movement. The Renaissance brought out an increased awareness of the written word across Europe and the number of people reading the Bible increased. With this awareness, many disapproved of the Catholic Church's unnecessary extravagance.

Beginning of the Protestant Reformation

During the Middle Ages, not many people other than priests knew the written word. With the Renaissance, however, many people learned to read and write. With the invention of the printing press, new ideas could be spread quickly and scriptures like the Bible were printed and distributed easily to people. Additionally, as the standard of living improved among the Europeans, they could afford to give their children a formal and thorough education.

It was during this time that a monk by the name of Martin Luther began to question the Catholic Church and its various practices. He made a list of 95 points, where he listed

Martin Luther's translation of the Bible into German.

the teachings of the Catholic church that differed from the Bible's written word and he highlighted where the Church had gone wrong. He published his writings as the *95 Theses* in 1517 and nailed it to the door of a Catholic Church.

The 95 Theses

The 95 points or theses were written by Martin Luther, a pastor at the University of Wittenberg. He was a monk and scholar who wrote a document that questioned the methods of the Church and asked for an explanation behind the "indulgences" of the Church, which told people that they would be forgiven if they paid money to the Church. The 95 theses stated that the Bible was the central authority when it came to religion and that people attained salvation through their faith, not their deeds. This was the basis for the Protestant Reformation.

Lutheran Church Dresden Frauenkirche in Dresden, Germany.

Reformation Movement, St. Peter's Basilica, Vatican City, Italy.

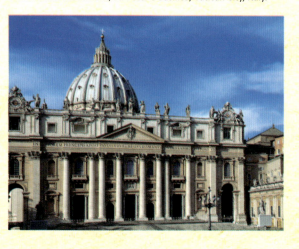

Counter Reformation

The Counter Reformation, also known as the Catholic Reformation or Catholic Revival, was the result of the efforts of the Roman Catholics against the Protestant Reformation, which started in the sixteenth and seventeenth centuries. It occurred around the same time as the Protestant Reformation.

Chiesa del Gesu Church built in the late sixteenth century by the Jesuits in Rome, Italy.

Internal calls for reform

Even within the Catholic Church, the reformation movement had brought about different views and new religious orders. Other groups were established and brought about another level of religious renewal; for instance, the Ursulines, Jesuits and Carmelite order. Pope Paul III was the first Pope to actually show some reaction to the Protestant movement. He called for the Council of Trent, where he tried to normalise the training of priests and requested for the prohibition of the luxurious living of the clergy. The Jesuits were founded in 1540 by St. Ignatius Loyola and were disbanded in 1773 by Pope Clement XIV. They were known for their role in education, missionary work and theology. Pope John Paul II constantly clashed with the Jesuits. He believed that they had become too political and leftist in their views.

The Roman inquisition

The Roman inquisition started in 1542 to counter dissent and could, to some extent, control the Protestant movement. It involved the army and political leaders against the protestant movement. In fact, the policies of Emperor Charles V and his son Philip II clearly reflect this. They were linked to the Spanish inquisition. The elements that came under direct attack due to the target of these inquisitions were the Virgin Mary, St. Peter, etc.

After-effects of Counter Reformation

The Counter Reformation brought about the standardisation of worship. Laws of the Church were reorganised and the life of clergies was brought under scrutiny. The movement brought many people back to the Catholic Church in Austria, Poland, Holland, Germany and Hungary. However, in England, the Counter Reformation movement took longer to be effective. The main players of this movement were Caesar Baronius, St. Robert Bellarmine, Pedro Calderón de la Barca, Richard Crashaw, St. Francis Borgia, Robert Southwell and Torquato Tasso.

FAST FACT

The Sack of Rome in 1527 by the troops of Charles V was enough to convince even the most confident of cardinals that it was dangerous to get involved in political gambles.

Portrait of Pope Paul III.

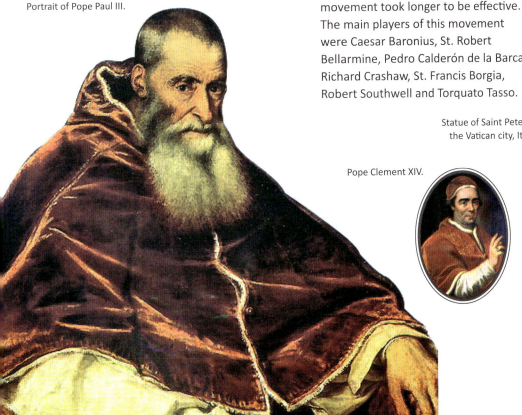

Statue of Saint Peter in the Vatican city, Italy.

Pope Clement XIV.

Aristocratic Revolt in France

Towards the end of the eighteenth century, King Louis XVI's investment towards the American Revolution left France's economy in shambles. The royal treasure was empty. For more than 20 years the country had suffered bad harvests. Inflation was at an all time high. This led to a feeling of great discontent among the peasants. Some resorted to rioting and looting. Others took to the streets and decided to revolt.

March of the women to Versailles, 1789.

Fiscal reforms

Around the time of the French Revolution, France was already going through a financial crisis. However, one of the triggers of the revolution actually occurred when Charles-Alexandre de Calonne, the controller general of finances, wanted to tax the privileged in order to deal with the budget shortage. He called for an assembly that consisted of the estates general, clergy and aristocracy, with very few representatives of the bourgeoisie and proposed his reforms to them. However, the assembly did not want to take responsibility of this. They suggested calling the Estates-General, who represented the clergy, the aristocracy and the Third Estate, which consisted of the commoners. This assembly had not met since 1614. However, this did not stop Calonne or his successors from trying to enforce their fiscal reforms, despite protests from different classes, which ultimately led to the aristocratic revolt.

Freedom of press

A lot had changed for France from 1614. There was a call for equal representation and the removal of the noble veto, which meant that everyone could vote, not just the nobility. This displeased the nobles. A public debate followed, but a stalemate stalled the proceedings.

Louis XVI reappointed Jacques Necker as the finance minister. The king also granted freedom to the press and there was printing material all over France regarding the rebuilding of the French State. On 26th August, 1789, the Declaration of the Rights of Man and of the Citizen was introduced, which claimed liberty, equality, inviolability of property and the right to resist oppression. On 5th October, 1789, Parisians marched to Versailles and brought the royal family back to Paris.

The Arc de Triomphe de l'Étoile in Paris, France.

A portrait of the Peasant War that called for the abolishment of the feudal system.

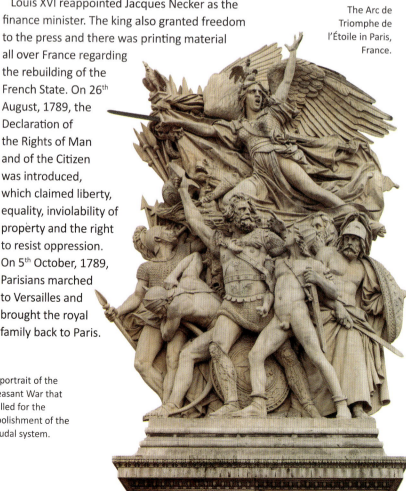

Tax payment

Louis XVI appointed Charles de Calonne as the controller general of finances in 1783. The French government approached various European banks for a loan, but because of its bad financial crisis it found no credibility and got no loan. Calonne saw taxation as a measure to save the country from financial disaster. He came up with an idea to extend taxation not just for peasants but also for the nobles and the members of the parliaments. At the Assembly of Notables, Calonne urged the nobles to either agree to the new taxes or to surrender their exemption to the already existing ones. The nobles refused both and opposed Calonne, who was dismissed shortly thereafter. The wealthy commoners or the bourgeoisie were hardworking, educated men who did not have titles like the elite and were, therefore, subjected to the same taxation as the poor peasants. The bourgeoisie would soon become the catalyst for the Revolution.

Alexandre de Calonne (1734–1802).

Aristocrates of France.

FAST FACT

The guillotine was a popular method of punishment during the French Revolution. It remained a legal form of execution in France right up till 1981!

Absolute rule

For many years prior to the French Revolution, the French royalty was corrupt and had a system of absolute rule. The local parliaments (provincial judicial boards), guilds or religious groups enforced laws. The royalty of the Bourbon dynasty, French nobles and clergy abused power during the late 1700s and the poor French peasantry were forced into feudal obligations. Heavy taxes were imposed on the working class in order to pay for the extravagances of the royalty. However, the peasants, who were a majority of the population, grew tired of being exploited. They were well aware of the situation and the unfairness of it all. Soon, they refused to pay taxes.

Empty treasury

The economic situation in France during the late 1700s had considerably worsened. It didn't help that the country was already suffering from a famine and cattle diseases, which made the agricultural yields poor, a condition that didn't bode well for France's large population.

Furthermore, France's prolonged involvement in the Seven Years' War of 1756-1763 and its participation in the American Revolution of 1775-1783 had brought the country to the brink of bankruptcy. To make matters worse, King Louis XVI lived an extravagant lifestyle that was funded by the people's taxes and Queen Marie Antoinette had frivolous spending habits, which only put more pressure on an already empty treasury. The people were frustrated by their conditions and it was this unrest that caused the great French Revolution.

Statues of King Louis XVI and Marie Antoinette from Saint Denis Basilica.

Events of 1789

Years of feudal oppression and economic problems led to the French Revolution. King Louis XVI's financial advisors reviewed the almost empty treasury and tried to increase the taxes. But this advice was not accepted and a controller general of finance, Charles de Calonne, was brought in. Calonne called for taxing the nobles. He suggested that, among other things, France begin taxing the previously exempt nobility. The nobility refused, even after Calonne pleaded with them during the Assembly of Notables in 1787. Financial ruin, thus, seemed imminent.

The voting process

The Estates General met in Versailles on 5th May, 1789. They wondered how the voting should progress by giving advantage to the majority of the population. The Third Estate was larger than the nobility and clergy but the Parlement of Paris ruled that each estate would receive only one vote irrespective of its size. This way, the Third Estate's vote was eventually overruled. This led to feuds that were incompatible and the Third Estate, which recognised the majority it enjoyed, unofficially declared itself as the sovereign National Assembly on June 17 of the same year. Just days after this announcement, quite a few members from the other two estates quickly shifted their loyalties over to the new revolutionary assembly.

The royal officials were not happy with this revolutionary assembly and chose to ban the deputies from attending their meeting by locking the hall on June 20. But that didn't stop the assembly, which gathered at the king's indoor tennis court and refused to leave until they were given the right to choose a new constitution for France. This was the first time that the French citizens publicly

Declaration of Rights, 1793.

revolted against their king. Due to this event, the king eventually gave in and asked the nobles and the rest of the clergy to join the assembly. This new formation was officially named the National Constituent Assembly on July 9.

Formation of a new constitution

In the countryside, peasants and farmers who were struggling against the feudal system, attacked the manors and big estates of landlords. These attacks were called the "Great Fear". The assembly released the declaration of the rights of citizens that put an appropriate judicial code in place to protect the autonomy of the French citizens.

The insurrection of the slaves of Santo Domingo in Paris. Free men entered the Convention and called for the abolition of slavery.

Declaration of Pillnitz of 1791.

Failure of the National Convention

The National Convention abolished the monarchy and declared France as a republic. The convention executed Louis XVI for treason in January 1793. The Committee of Public Safety's performance was poor and it did not help that the war with Austria and Prussia did not end well for France. The Montagnards and Girondins opposed each other, and that took centre stage in the first phase of the Convention, which was from September 1792 to May 1793. The Montagnards were in favour of granting the poor class some political power, but were opposed by the Girondins, who wanted a more bourgeoisie representation. Soon, the Montagnards controlled the Convention's second phase. Unhappy with the Girondins, angry French citizens led the convention and the Jacobins under Maximilien de Robespierre took over.

The short-lived peace

Although the national assembly managed to draft a constitution, the peace of the moment was temporary, because differences between the moderates and radical assembly members slowly arose. Shortly, the common folk, including workers and labourers, started feeling ignored and their opinions were not being considered. Thus, while a few wanted constitutional monarchies to continue, there were others who wanted the monarchy out of the country. The Hapsburgs feared that a similar revolution would spark off in Prussia and they announced the Declaration of Pillnitz, which was brought out by the Hapsburg Holy Roman Emperor Leopold II and Frederick William II of Prussia. This declared that both the Roman Empire and Prussian King were against the French Revolution.

Attempt for a stable economy

Robespierre tried to implement laws to stabilise the economy, but somewhere, the fear of counter-revolutionary forces made him a little obsessed and he started a reign of terror. There was a time from 1793 to 1794 when he executed more than 15,000 people at the guillotine.

Maximilien de Robespierre

1789: Formation of the National Assembly

1793: Execution of Louis XVI

FAST FACT

Did you know that while the peasants had to pay taxes to the nobles, the Church and the king, the nobles themselves didn't have to pay taxes at all?

Execution of King Louis XVI in January 1793 during the French Revolution.

New French Regime

On 4th August, the Assembly adopted the Declaration of the Rights of Man and of the Citizen, also known as the *Déclaration des droits de l'homme et du citoyen*, which was a statement of democratic principles based on the philosophical and political ideas of Renaissance thinkers, such as Jean-Jacques Rousseau. It was committed to the replacement of the ancient regime with one that focussed on equal opportunity, freedom of speech, sovereignty and, most importantly, a representative government.

Declaration of the Rights of Man and of the Citizen in 1789.

Attack on monarchy

The Declaration was an open attack on the monarchy and strongly opposed their regime. It wanted to base the element of equality before the law and aimed to replace the system that existed under the monarchy. Despite limitations in the aims of the declaration, this Declaration of the Rights of Man and of the Citizen was recognised as the "credo of the new age" by famous historian Jules Michelet.

Menus-Plaisirs hotel, Versailles, France—seat of French National Constituent Assembly in 1789.

Formation of the formal constitution

Drafting a formal constitution was quite a demanding task for the National Constituent Assembly, which was already reeling under the pressure of the adverse economic times that the country had been facing.

For many months, the Assembly argued on questions such as who would be accountable for electing delegates. Would the clergy owe loyalty to the Roman Catholic Church or the French government? How much authority would continue to remain with the king? The first written constitution went with the moderate voices of the assembly and put a constitutional monarchy in place. According to this, the monarch would get royal veto power and would also be allowed to appoint ministers.

This negotiation, with its moderate thinking, could not be accepted by radical leaders like Maximilien de Robespierre, Camille Desmoulins and Georges Danton, who started advocating public opinion towards a republican form of government and the trial of Louis XVI.

A 1789 cover page from Robespierre's book.

Reign of terror

The execution of the king was not the most violent phase of the revolution. After the divisions in the National Convention, the most violent phase of French history was only just beginning. In 1793, the Jacobins seized control of the National Convention and brought in radical measures, including putting a new calendar in place and abolishing Christianity. Noting the chaos and disorder in and around France, Jacobin, the foremost political party, were steadfast in their approach to squash any resistance. Neighbourhood watches were made to seek the people who were not loyal to the Jacobin stance. The 10-month period was the reign of terror; it was supervised and directed by the Committee of Public Safety, a committee of 12 leaders that also included Maximilien de Robespierre. Alleged enemies of the revolution were guillotined under the draconian Committee of Public Safety. During this period, thousands of innocent people were tortured and put to death, sometimes solely for having a diverse political opinion.

The Jacobin's Fountain in Lyon, France.

A guillotine used during the executions.

1795: France's first bicameral legislature

1799: Napoleon Bonaparte is France's first consul

First bicameral legislature

The National Convention, which comprised the Girondins, approved a new constitution in August, 1795, thus creating France's first bicameral legislature. The creation of this legislature meant that the executive power would lie in the hands of a five-member directory or the "directoire". This directory was appointed by the Parliament.

Royalists and Jacobins protested the new regime, but were rapidly silenced by the army that was led by a young general named Napoleon Bonaparte.

The Directory

The Directory went through a host of problems in its four years of power. It faced financial disasters, popular discontent, incompetence and political corruption. By the 1790s, the directors were relying heavily on the army to sustain their power.

On 9th November, 1799, a young general by the name of Napoleon Bonaparte staged a coup and abolished the Directory. He appointed himself France's "first consul" and went on to become one of the most famous leaders in the history of France.

Napoleon Bonaparte

Monnet's illustrations of the night of privilege abolition.

FAST FACT

Before the revolutionaries took over the country of France, both Protestant and Jewish religions were illegal in France!

French Reign of Terror

Bataille of Fleurus 1794.

Other countries looked upon the French revolution with renewed hope. Switzerland, the United Provinces and Belgium in particular were impressed with the French Revolution. But counter revolutionaries comprising nobles left the struggle, abandoned their country and moved away. The "émigrés", as they were called, formed armed or unarmed groups and asked for support from European leaders.

France declares war on Austria

The war between France and Austria was a pure political move made by the rulers of France in order to "exploit the revolution". The King, Louis XVI, his supporting monarchs and other officials wanted to start a war so that it would increase the popularity of the king among the people. Although some people in his court felt that at the time France was too weak to win a war. They were worried that an unwanted war would increase the intensity of the revolution brewing between the people. Some believed that the revolution would increase the influence of the military and the monarchy but anger the people of Austria and other European countries. Upon the death of the Austrian Emperor, Leopold II, France declared a war against Austria on 20th April, 1972. Prussia joined Austria in the war. France won the war against Austria by defeating the Prussian and Austrian army. This gave them the confidence to wage more wars against European powers.

Statue on top of the Monument aux Girondins on Place des Quinconces, Bordeaux, France.

With Austria's defeat, France was able to take over the Austrian Netherlands. This upset Britain and the Dutch Republic who did not want Netherlands to come into the hands of France. France also waged a war with Belgium and Rhineland in 1792. Meanwhile the French Revolution was still brewing and the people of France believed King Louis XVI to be weak and indecisive. He was beheaded in 1973 and Marie Antoinette, his wife, was executed a few months after that. Meanwhile, Britain, Austria and Prussia formed a coalition known as the "First Coalition". Spain and some other European powers joined in and they waged a war on France. As a result, the French faced many defeats and the troops stationed in the newly conquered territories were forced to make a hasty retreat. Within France, its people were conducting revolts against the republican regime of France.

An illustration showing Marie Antoinette before her execution.

The Montagnards vs Girondins

In the Legislative Assembly, the Girondists were the voice of the democratic revolution and were useful in furthering it. They managed to get the king to agree to a ministry comprising Roland, Dumouriez and Servan who supported the revolution. Shortly after, a war was declared against Austria. The Montagnards and Girondists were opposed to the monarchy. Both sides had monarchs, republicans and democrats who did not want to break the unity of France. When the First Coalition made matters worse, the Montagnards who had the support of workers, craftsmen and shopkeepers seized power and brought in liberal, economic and social policies to appease their support base. These policies ensured that the rich were heavily taxed. They provided assistance to the needy and disabled. Education was to be compulsory and free for all.

Ronot Charles, the last of the Montagnards.

Wars of Vendee

One of the policies was to sell the properties of the émigré. Such policies saw stiff opposition and aggressive reactions. The wars in Vendee and other uprisings in Provence, Normandy, Lyon and Bordeaux served as a response to these policies. The reign of terror managed to change things around with the arrest of more than 300,000 suspects. This brought the uprisings to a halt, with more than 17,000 executions, some without a trial.

The Battle of Le Mans was a battle in the Wars of Vendee.

The government in place raised an army of a million men and fought with the Austrians to regain Belgium. The victory made the restrictions seem futile and Robespierre was overthrown and executed in 1794. The Maximum Policy was eliminated. The idea of economic equality was abandoned and the National Convention discussed if a new constitution was required. In 1795, Napoleon Bonaparte crushed another attempt by royalists to seize power and detached the National Convention.

A Girondins monument from 1902 in the city of Bordeaux.

1792: France declares a war on Austria

1795: National Convention is detached

FAST FACT

The agitators of the revolution began to spread a false tale about Marie Antoinette. In this tale, when Marie Antoinette was told that people had no bread, she remarked, "Let them eat cake!"

Napoleon Bonaparte

Napoleon Bonaparte, also known as the "Little Corporal", became the French general, first consul (1799–1804) and also the emperor of the French (1804–1814/15). He became an important personality in the country's history. Being from the army, his major interests lay in strengthening the army and that's just what he did. He managed to transform the French military. He initiated the Napoleonic Code, a great example of the civil-law code. He also rationalised education.

Napoleon Bonaparte becomes a national hero

While fighting against Austria in 1796, Napoleon took over the command of the French army. Upon his arrival in Italy, he realised that the French army was losing to the Austrian army as most of them had died, were wounded or sick. He re-organised the army and ordered the troops. He was an efficient leader. He wanted to have more soldiers than the enemy. He called for help when needed and kept the spirit of the troops up. Soon the Austrians were forced to leave Italy. When the victory was announced back home, Napoleon was hailed as a national hero. Napoleon became first consul at the age of 30. In December 1799, his plea for peace with Britain and Austria was rejected. During the 1800s, he launched a surprise attack on Austria in the Battle of Marengo. The Austrian army was defeated and the Austrian Emperor, Francis II, had to agree to sign the Treaty of Luneville in 1801. England too fell in line and signed a peace agreement with France called the "Peace of Amiens".

Napoleon crossing the Alps.

First consul

In 1802, Napoleon proclaimed himself "First Consul for Life", which stood for a legislated succession to rule for his son. Despite the fact that he had no sons and being the first consul, he was the most powerful, yet he was very wary. To keep the charade of a republic, he set up imaginary representatives, including a legislative body and council of notables, which in reality were powerless. Napoleon sold the French territory of Louisiana to the newly independent USA in 1803 for 80 million francs, which was referred to as the "Louisiana Purchase".

Louisiana state quarter coin and old French coins used in 1856.

Napoleon the leader

He demonstrated great prowess in restoring peace and order after the French Revolution. He had worked very hard to gain the support of the Royalist faction. He tried to improve relations with the Catholic Church as Catholicism remained the religion of the majority. He signed a Concordat with Pope Pius VII, as per which the Church officially recognised the French Republic and returned the property that it had taken during the Revolution. In return, Napoleon announced that Catholicism was the official religion of the Republic of France.

Pope Pius VII

Battle of Marengo.

The Napoleonic code

There was a demand for such a code in France during the time of the French Revolution. Napoleon already had the base of the code, he simply needed to add details. Under the Napoleonic Code, all male citizens were perceived to be equal whether rich or poor. The previous French traditions of class over mass, privileges to the rich and hereditary nobility were removed. All male citizens had freedom to property, person and contract. They were able to enjoy civil rights. The dissolution of marriage by terms of divorce or annulment was also discussed. However, such rights of women

The Napoleonic Code in Speyer, Historical Museum of the Palatinate.

were granted to the father or husband, or the male that controlled the property.

1799: Napoleon is a national hero

1803: Napoleon sells the territory of Louisiana

FAST FACT

"Napoleon complex" is a psychological condition where short people become defensive due to their height. It was named after Napoleon because he was incorrectly believed to be 5 feet 2 inches when actually he was 5 feet 6 inches.

The Napoleonic Era

Napoleon wanted to establish a French-dominated empire in Europe and ruled for 15 years. His family was wealthy and he received an excellent education. He later attended a military academy in France and became the second lieutenant in an artillery regiment. He returned to Corsica (captured by France) when his father died. He soon consolidated his power and gave himself the title of Emperor. He was always at war with Prussia, Austria and Britain. Until 1812, France won all the wars under his leadership as he had great tact and could turn the fate of a losing battle. Napoleon's strategy was to annex territories and set up smaller kingdoms in parts of Germany, Italy, Poland and Spain.

Napoleon abdicates

Napoleon's regime brought about many changes in the country that included everyone being equal before the law; he made the bureaucracy very strict by having able bureaucrats to handle those duties. The educational institutions that Napoleon started gave specialised technical training. Despite the fact that he made certain announcements on accord of the Roman Catholic Church, but overall during his period religious freedom survived. During his era, he managed to destroy the old regime in Belgium, western Germany and northern Italy.

The era of Napoleon

Napoleon won many battles against Austria and Italy. He wanted to take over the world and fought many battles for France. He would collect tax from the territories he conquered in other nations. This tax money was used to repair France's failing economy. Therefore, Napoleon focussed on winning the battles he fought against Italy and Austria. He sent money and gold back to France. In 1798, he tried to find passage to India through Egypt but was defeated by Admiral Nelson of Britain.

Napoleon went on to become one of the most important figures in the history of France due to his dedication towards his country.

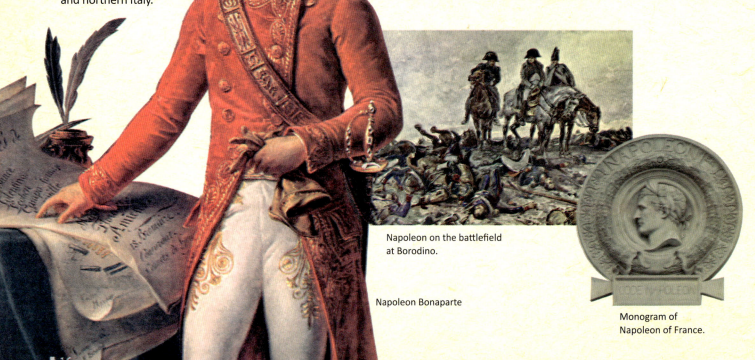

Napoleon on the battlefield at Borodino.

Napoleon Bonaparte

Monogram of Napoleon of France.

Battle of Waterloo 1815.

Napoleon is abdicated

In the period between 1803 and 1815, France was engaged in several wars, called "Napoleonic Wars", with many European nations like Britain, Austria and Russia. He then began to wage a large-scale economic war against Britain in 1806 called the "Continental System". Russia backed out of this system and Napoleon decided to attack Russia. Instead of responding, the Russian troops kept retreating and Napoleon's soldiers were forced to trek deeper into Russia with diminishing resources. Russia then invaded France during the Peninsular War. Thus, Napoleon's army lost many battles at the same time against Prussia, Britain, Russia, Sweden and Austria. Napoleon was forced to abdicate and was exiled to a coast of Italy.

Hundred Days campaign

On 6th April, 1814, Napoleon was exiled to Elba, a Mediterranean island. It was a small island and Napoleon was allowed to rule over it. His wife and son were sent to Austria. Napoleon, now in his mid-40s, was as determined now as when he first became the Emperor of France. With support from more than one thousand people, Napoleon escaped from Elba to return to Paris. Here, his loyal supporters and citizens welcomed him back. The new king, Louis XVIII, fled in fear. Napoleon began his Hundred Days campaign. He groomed a new army. Meanwhile, the leaders of Britain, Prussia, Russia and Austria prepared to get rid of Napoleon once and for all. Napoleon started the campaign in 1815 by invading Belgium. The British and Prussian armies were present here. The Battle of Ligny in Prussia saw Napoleon defeat the troops. The next battle, the Battle of Waterloo, was fought in Brussels where Napoleon was defeated and forced to abdicate once again.

After the Napoleonic Era

After Napoleon was exiled, the allied powers and remaining leaders of the French republic came together to try and restore Europe to what it was before Napoleon. However, some nations took advantage by trying to invade and conquer territories. Prussia invaded new territories in western Germany. Russia took over Poland and Britain took over the French, Spanish and Dutch colonies. A new monarchy was put into place.

FAST FACT

Napoleon was first married to Josephine de Beauharnais, a widow who was six years older. A childless marriage resulted in the marriage being annulled. Napoleon had many illegitimate children.

Congress of Vienna, conference to organise Europe after the defeat of Napoleon, 1815.

Industrial Revolution

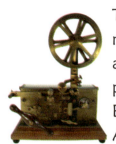

The Industrial Revolution altered the procedure of manufacturing different items. New machines were invented around the 1700s and by the 1800s, it was possible to mass produce certain items with the use of machinery. Starting in Britain, this revolution quickly spread to Europe and North America bringing about an age of urbanisation with it.

About the revolution

The Industrial Revolution took place between the eighteenth and nineteenth centuries. At the beginning of the revolution, the European nations practiced agriculture. All nations had predominantly rural societies. It was during this revolution that the US and the nations of Europe developed urban and industrial practices. Then it spread to the rest of the world. A historian named Arnold Toynbee first used the term "Industrial Revolution" to show England's economic development.

Technological revolution

The use of iron and steel as raw materials, the discovery of new sources of energy such as fuel and coal as well as improved transportation such as with the steam engine kick-started the industrialisation of Europe. The invention of machines like the spinning jenny and power loom allowed for mass production which took less time than manual labour. The factory system came into existence. Means of communication also improved with the introduction of the radio and telegraph. Industries began to use scientific knowledge to improve their products and come up with more uses for raw materials.

Other changes in society

The earliest effects of such technological changes were seen in the production of agricultural materials. This allowed people to make more money all round which ensured a wider distribution of wealth. Now, man stopped looking at agricultural land as a source of wealth and began to think of other ways to earn. It helped develop the working class who were free to think of other things besides work and money.

The Industrial Revolution was a time of invention.

FAST FACT

Two men named William Cooke and Charles Wheatstone introduced the first commercial electrical telegraph. Now, to communicate with each other, people could use the telegraph.

First Industrial Revolution

The Industrial Revolution first began in Britain in 1760 and was contained there until 1830. This gave the British an edge they wanted to preserve. So, they banned the export of skilled labourers, machinery or techniques of manufacture. Also, wealthy men from other countries hoped to bring the big secret to their countries. As a result, the Industrial Revolution moved to Belgium thanks to two Englishmen, William and John Cockerill, who started machine shops there. Then came the Agricultural Revolution where farmers were replaced by machines and had to find jobs in towns.

1760: Start of the Industrial Revolution in Britain

1807: Industrial Revolution comes to Belgium

A steam engine with the intricate parts below.

New inventions

The textile industry improved with inventions like the Spinning Jenny by James Hargreaves and the Spinning Mule by Samuel Crompton. Henry Cort came up with the puddling process which was used to make wrought iron. James Watt enhanced the efficiency of steam engines on a design developed by Thomas Savery and Thomas Newcomen.

A cotton mill in Lancashire, England using power looms in 1835.

Rest of Europe slowly joins in on the Industrial bandwagon

When Britain was undergoing vast industrial developments, France was immersed in the Revolution and its indecisive political situation discouraged people from making large investments towards industrial developments. It was only in 1840s that France joined in and despite having had great developments it lagged behind England. Germany started its industrial development only after 1870 and it grew so rapidly that it became the world leader in many industries. In Asia, Japan joined in this revolution. Soon, Soviet Union, China and India also became industrialised by the mid twentieth century.

Effects of Industrial Revolution

The Industrial Revolution radically altered the social structure of England. People from all classes gained education and became literate. With better living conditions, life expectancy improved and the population began to grow. The roles of men and women began to change as women entered factories as workers. At the beginning though, women were urged to stay home and men were paid higher wages than female workers.

A typical family scene in eighteenth century Britain.

Growing population

The population in the industrial nations began to grow faster than ever. This was the result of various reasons. Firstly, there was a sharp drop in the death rate as more food became available. Also, fewer plagues and epidemics broke out as people began to eat healthier diets. The birth rate also increased. Younger generations earned higher wages and were able to marry and produce children earlier.

The Industrial Revolution saw an improvement in the medicines available.

Growth of the working class

The literacy rate increased due to an increase in the number of private schools. Also books, newspapers and journals were now mass produced at a quicker rate. This was because printing presses began to use machines like the Gutenberg Press. With the use of machines, work was done faster which gave people leisure time. Higher wages meant money for hobbies. So, people began to read newspapers and books. As a result, they began to think and form opinions about the society. Workers became aware of their conditions. Rural workers started moving towards cities to get jobs and earn more money.

Gender bias

Prior to the Industrial Revolution, gender roles were different, because both men and women worked together in the cottage industries. Businesses were mostly home run. Farmers involved their entire families, thus making it a "family business". Women were deprived of any social, political or economic rights outside their home. Women could not vote or even own property. The "rule of thumb" was a cruel law that found tacit support by the courts and referred to the rule that a man could beat his wife, with a stick so long as the stick was not bigger than the width of his thumb.

FAST FACT

The mid-1700s saw England producing cotton cloth. The spinning of cotton into thread on a spinning wheel was the first thing that launched England into the Industrial Revolution. Since such spinning and weaving were done in homes, they were called cottage industries.

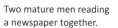

Two mature men reading a newspaper together.

Metal factories mostly employed men as they were believed to be stronger.

Change in gender roles

As most businesses were run from homes, there was no difference between work and home life. This changed with the Industrial Revolution where men, women and even children worked in factories or mills. Men were paid more than women and children. The working hours were long. After many years, the government tried to eradicate child labour, even as the working hours for women were reduced. Many women left the workforce to take care of their homes and children. Men became the breadwinners of the family. The roles formed by the Industrial Revolution came to dictate the perceptions of men and women, as these gender roles remained the same for the next generations.

Female labourers working in a factory.

Transformation of transportation

With the mass production of goods and raw materials came the need for better modes of transport. The Industrial Revolution saw stronger and more reliable roads, the building of canals and the introduction of railway lines. Raw materials were now transported using faster means. Manufacturers were also able to find and travel to new markets. This not only helped spread wealth to other parts, but also helped introduce the industrial revolution to faraway places.

A costly affair

With rapid industrialisation and urbanisation, heavy, bulky raw materials like iron and coal were required, but transporting them was a costly affair. The demand for coal also increased. Its transportation was difficult and it was a very expensive resource. Goods were earlier transported by water. With the construction of canals, waterways were expanded and improved and more places could be reached by water. With steam engines and locomotives, the use of horse-drawn carriages was limited to private use and for short distances.

The Industrial Revolution saw the invention of steamboats, cars and aeroplanes.

Social Impact of the Industrial Revolution

With the introduction of factories, people's lives slowly changed. People moved from rural areas to cities in search of work. Cities grew and expanded while villages were deserted. Urbanisation set in. Workers spent hours at factories and were closely supervised by their foremen. Disagreements between workers and supervisors arose. Many social evils were introduced.

A photo of a city in Britain in the early nineteenth century.

Britain gains economical supremacy

Many technological innovations took place in Britain during the Industrial Revolution. Thus, it became the epicentre of industrialisation. It also helped that Britain had a greater supply of coal which increased the production of iron. Although France had plenty of wood, it had very little coal. Holland was able to produce peat but needed every other material to carry out a large-scale production of iron. Being an island country, Britain also had water transportation that aided in its trading with the market overseas.

So, while it is said that in the eighteenth century, both France and Britain were at par with each other, the French revolution gave Britain the chance to supersede France and become the new leader of Europe. It also helped that they had a huge head start.

Employment of cheap labour

Owners of industries were looking at the best way to maximise their profits. Machines were doing everything, so factories employed unskilled workers. Children were employed for this reason. In fact, an entire family worked in the same factory, especially a poor family. Most factories had 15-hour working days which was not suitable for children. These conditions led to many people falling sick or dying. Housing conditions were yet to be improved and would see improvement nearly half a century later.

FAST FACT

In the 1860s, around one-fifth of the workers in British factories were under the age of 15. They worked long hours in highly dangerous conditions.

1760: Start of the Industrial Revolution

20th century: USA is leading in industrialisation

Factories would release a lot of harmful gases into the environment.

Introduction of Laws

Around the 1700s, the conditions of workers were exposed and the British Parliament introduced laws that limited working hours and prohibited the employment of children, especially very young children. It was around the same time that Charles Dickens published his novels on the suffering of child labourers. People began to fight for child rights and protested against factories. Workers also joined these protests and spoke about their conditions.

Oliver Twist was one such novel where a child is employed in a workshop.

Photo of a workshop with young boys.

Migration to cities

With the Industrial Revolution, Britain saw an increase in cities and big towns which had factories, both big and small. The population increased from 8 million in 1801 to over 40 million in 1901. Cities expanded and people migrated from villages in search of work. They mostly ended up working in factories. Men, women and children began to work in factories and even in the hot, unhealthy work environment of coal mines. The cost of labour for factories was now very cheap. Owners of such establishments grew rich fast, while the labourers were very poor and lived in slums.

Social and economic thoughts during the mercantilism

The Industrial Revolution dominantly followed mercantilism which believed that resources were limited and one had to control these resources. Economists and thinkers like Adam Smith and Jeremy Bentham came up with many theories and ways to promote and follow mercantilism. Bentham proposed that all the models be it social, economic or political should ultimately be only about bringing happiness for people.

FAST FACT

Even though the Industrial Revolution came to the US much later than it came to Britain, by the twentieth century the US became the world's leading industrial nation.

Battersea Power Station, London, UK.

Revolutions of 1848

1848, French revolutionaries burning the royal carriages at the Chateau d'Eu.

There were a series of revolutions that began against royalty and monarchs, but particularly against the monarchies in Europe. The revolutions of 1848 commenced with Sicily and soon spread to Germany, France, Italy and even Austria. These revolutions were mostly unsuccessful.

Poor economic conditions

Between 1845 and 1846, all of Europe was facing economic crises. Poor grain harvests, constant battles, high death rates and other such factors contributed to the poor and depressing economic conditions. There was a shortage of food, so food prices were high. The rate of employment and opportunities for labour were less. People began to resent the monarchs and nobles for their high status

Guardhouse students of 1848 were the springs of the revolutionary movement.

and comfortable lives. All this led to terrible unrest which ended up creating the Revolutions of 1848 across Europe, except for Russia.

Revolts galore

The Italian revolution started around 1848 in Sicily. The idea of holding revolts soon moved to France. However, it did not spread to Russia, Spain and Scandinavia. In England, there were some protests and demonstrations held in Ireland but it did not manifest to anything more than that. Revolts also broke out in Holland, Belgium and Denmark, but they ended with peaceful negotiations and useful reforms.

The Working Class Revolts

The revolution seemed to gain attention and victories in France. There were many differences of opinions. This led to the "Workers' Insurrection" in June, 1848. The Austrian monarchy braved the protests, while in Prussia King William IV led a movement for the unification of Germany. But France did not lend its support to the revolutionaries in Europe.

Statue of King William IV, Greenwich.

Use of Force to Suppress Revolutions

The Revolution of 1848 was a liberal, nationalist movement that had taken over pretty much the whole of Europe. It was seen as the first protest against capitalism. Soon, countries from other nations followed suit. In Europe, these revolutions were called the "Spirit of 1848". Constitution-led governments were formed in unified Germany and Italy, and much later in all of Europe.

A picture depicting the three types of revolutionaries of 1848.

1848: Start of the European revolutions

1852: Napoleon III takes over France

Napoleon III and empress Eugenie entrance in Saint-Malo through triumphal arch, 1858.

Repression

Monarchs and other rulers used the nation's armies to repress the revolts and the insurgents. This was seen in France, then was followed by the Czechs in Prague and also by the Austrian army in Lombardy and Vienna. The Berlin and Prussian armies followed later. In fact, the French intervened to set things in order while this was done in Rome. The King of Prussia tried to unite Germany via a union of the German Princes. Austria and Russia, asked him to discard this idea and the same was discussed at the Convention of Olmütz in 1850.

FAST FACT

"Prussia" refers to areas of eastern and central Europe, respectively, which came under the Polish and German rule during the Middle Ages.

Results of the clampdown of revolts

The results of such shutting down of revolts were that the liberal democratic concessions that were granted earlier were withdrawn. Now, absolute monarchy was re-established in countries like Italy, Germany and Austria. The governments in agreement with the middle class and clergy, who felt threatened by the socialist ideology, strengthened their police forces. The freedom of press was restricted. In France, there was a coup against the assembly, when in 1852 Napoleon III took over the reins. The uprisings spread to the parliamentary governments. Austria came back to power over Hungary and drove the Sardinians away from Lombardy and Venice. Liberals, republicans and socialists across Europe either sought refuge in the US or went into hiding.

The Bundestag in Frankfurt.

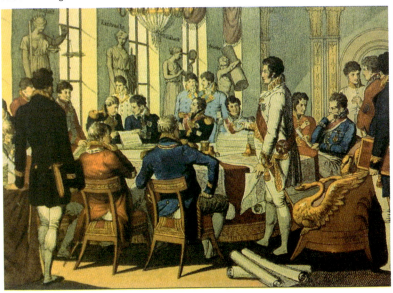

Romanticism

The word "romance" stood for many things. During the Middle Ages, romance was a style of writing found in stories, prose and poems which was used to refer to the heroic deeds of knights and soldiers. This changed with time, when it referred to a type of narrative in prose which had a unique, imaginative and unrealistic manner. "Romanticism" was a cultural movement that started in Europe. It was a reaction to the Industrial Revolution.

The House of the Seven Gables in Massachusetts is a 1668 colonial mansion. It was made famous by the American author, Nathaniel Hawthorne.

Spread to other fields

Hawthorne's "House of Seven Gables" is often referred to as an example of romance. Romanticism was actually a movement that started in the eighteenth century and continued to the nineteenth century. It had its traces in the fields of art, philosophy, religion, literature and even politics. This was a popular technique of art and method of writing.

Characteristics of Romanticism

The many characteristic elements of Romanticism include a deep admiration for natural beauty, an emphasis on emotion over logic and feelings over common sense and an internalising of the self. It was the largest artistic movement of the late 1700s and it influenced artists and writers across the continents. Poets and artists fostered individualism and idealism. It was also about actual emotion and passion. There was awareness towards mysticism and the supernatural.

Poets of this movement

Many poets embraced the Romantic Movement. Fredrich Schiller and Johann Wolfgang von Goethe being two examples. Wordsworth, Coleridge, Shelley, Keats and Lord Byron from England took the movement forward. Noted poet and writer Victor Hugo also contributed to the movement. Among the American poets, Walt Whitman and Edgar Allan Poe became the faces of the Romantic Movement in the US.

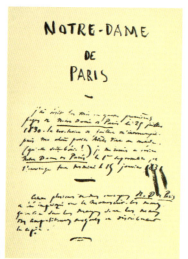

Notre-Dame de Paris, by Victor Hugo. Title of the original manuscript, 1829.

A monument of Victor Hugo in Paris, France.

FAST FACT

Did you know that the famous composer Ludwid van Beethoven gained his popularity during the Romantic period?

Nathaniel Hawthorne's "The Scarlett Letter," and "The House of the Seven Gables" became symbols of the Romantic Movement.

Statue of Johann Wolfgang von Goethe, poet, novelist, playwright and German scientist who introduced the Romantic Movement in Germany.

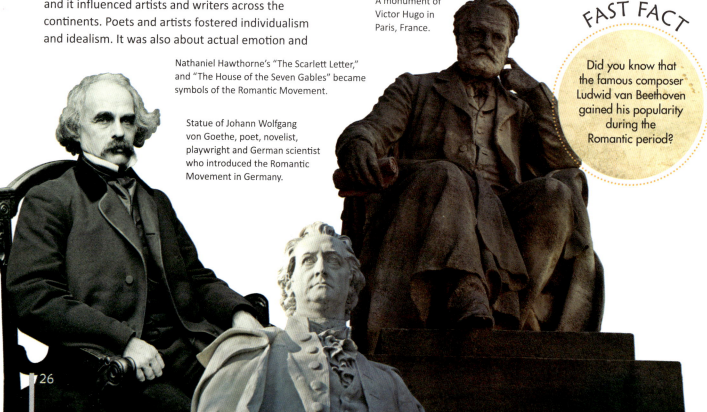

Romanticism and the Writers and Poets

The characteristic attitude of Romantic Age consisted of a heightened appreciation of natural beauty, a preference of emotion over reason and of feelings over intellect. By the eighteenth century, the words "romantique" and "romantic" came to be used in French and English, respectively, and meant magical, dramatic and astonishing. German poets and critics August Wilhelm and Friedrich Schlegel named this movement.

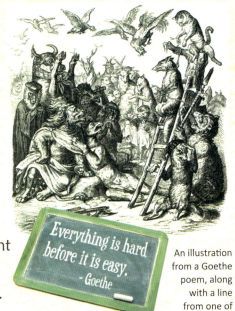

Everything is hard before it is easy.
- Goethe

An illustration from a Goethe poem, along with a line from one of his works.

Celebration of creativity

The writers of the Romantic Movement, as it is sometimes referred to, celebrated imagination, followed their intuition and were spontaneous. They believed in subjectivity, revolutionary thought, individualism and democracy. This was visible in the work done by Goethe, a German writer. Friedrich Hölderlin, Jean Paul, Novalis, Ludwig Tieck, Friedrich Schlegel, Wilhelm Heinrich Wackenroder and Friedrich Schelling were some other popular German writers. Poets like Vicomte de Chateaubriand, Charles Baudelaire and Rainer Maria Rilke, though not actively participating in this movement, were influenced by its ideologies. This was obvious from their work. Also, the ballads composed by English lyrical writers showed traces of this ideology.

Second phase

The second phase of Romanticism started in 1805 and lasted until the 1830s. It inspired cultural nationalism and a renewed reflection to national identity. It celebrated folklore, folk ballads, poetry, folk dance and folk music.

Romantic writers and poets

Sir Walter Scott was one of the first writers to have been interested in German Romanticism. He translated the works of some German poets and authors. He later moved on to historical novels and is said to be the inventor of them. Lord Byron, Shelley and Keats popularised the romantic poems. Authors also wrote on supernatural and grotesque themes. Mary Shelley's *Frankenstein* is a popular work of this period. Poets like William Wordsworth and Samuel Taylor Coleridge, poet and painter William Blake became examples of Romantic sensibility in Britain. German artists such as Caspar David and Friedrich Johann were celebrated for their works.

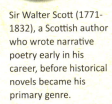

Sir Walter Scott (1771-1832), a Scottish author who wrote narrative poetry early in his career, before historical novels became his primary genre.

Hermann and Dorothea, characters of a Goethe poem.

Romanticism in the Arts

Venice - The Dogana and San Giorgio Maggiore by J. M. W. Turner

The Romanticists believed that every person had a right to life, liberty and equal opportunity. These ideas found their way to the American Declaration of Independence. The Romantic Movement was innately against industrialisation due to its social and ecological impacts. Romanticism revived peoples' concern for nature. Interest in old legends and folk ballads soon grew and writers used these elements in their writings as well.

1800: Beginning of the Romantic Era

1850: Decline of the Romantic Era

Emotions on canvas

The Romantic Age inspired artists to display their emotions on the canvas. Artists began to depict a scene based on their feelings towards a theme or a subject. This brought mood to an art piece. The movement gave wings to the imagination of the artists. It motivated the artist to delve into the spiritual world. The themes ranged from landscapes to religion. It was not about brush strokes, but about what feeling the art evoked. Precision was not the key, but emotion was.

Romanticism and the artwork

Caspar Friedrich's, *The Wanderer above the Sea of Fog* is one of the paintings that belonged to the realm of the Romantic Movement. The image of a man standing at a precipice of a hill with his back to the viewer is a great metaphor on man and the meaning of his existence in nature. Francisco Goya's *Third of May 1808* depicted the emotions of the Spanish resistance against Napoleon's army. The painting was among the first on war and its devastation.

The Wanderer above the Sea of Fog by Caspar Friedrich.

Other artists of the Romantic Movement

Other artists who contributed to the Romantic Era include Thomas Cole, the American artist who was known for his painting of landscapes. He was also the founder of the art movement in Hudson River School. Among the English artists were John Constable, Henry Fuseli and J.M.W. Turner. Their works represented the elements of romanticism. The other European Romantic artists were Eugene Delacroix, Thomas Gainsborough, Caspar Friedrich and Goya.

Art movement at the Hudson River School

The American Romantic artists were all about meticulous and romanticised landscapes. Most of them came from the Hudson River School. They were guided by Thomas Cole, who painted his first landscape at the Catskill Mountains. The Hudson River School was America's first artistic fraternity and it identified a group of city-based landscape painters from New York. In 1848 after Cole's death, Asher B. Durand led this movement. He soon became the president of the National Academy of Design.

Eugene Delacroix's painting depicting Henri IV conferring the regency upon Marie de' Medici.

Neoclassicism

Neoclassicism was an artistic style that began in the late eighteenth and early nineteenth centuries. The Neoclassical Movement was often described as a counterpart opposing Romanticism. It focussed on reviving the old forms of classical art used in Greece and Rome. It started from Rome and then spread to England, Sweden and Russia. The famous neoclassical painters of that time included Jacques-Louis David, Angelica Kauffmann, Jean-Auguste-Dominique Ingres and Anton Raphael Mengs. The noteworthy sculptors and architects of the neoclassical movement included Houdon, Canova, Mansart, Soufflot and John Nash among others. Neoclassicism is appreciated even today.

An example of Neoclassical art.

Jacques-Louis David's Portrait of Mrs Serizy.

Reaction to art

Neoclassicism was seen as a reaction to the Baroque and Rococo form of art and brought back the old formal architectural styles. France had a great influence on this art movement which then spread to England and Germany. This form of decorative art was popularised by kings and soon the styles came to known as Jacobean, Charles II, William and Mary, Queen Anne and Georgian. Robert Adam, an architect was someone who also used this form for his furniture, carpets and other accessories. Towards the end of the movement, Neoclassicism became a topic exploited by political, economic, spiritual and social reformists. It was seen as a cure to religious fanaticism.

Designed by Robert Adam in 1774 in the Palladian style, Pulteney Bridge crosses the River Avon in Bath, England, UK.

Bust of Jean Auguste Dominique Ingres.

Realism

Realism was an artistic technique which looked at a subject or theme in a straight and realistic manner, without the rules of artistic theory. Realism was a reaction to the over-the-top nature of Romanticism. Some paintings that depicted realism can be found in Copley and Goya's works. Realism started as a movement in France with artists like Camille Corot and Jean Millet. American painters like Eakins and Ossawa Tanner were also influenced by realism, which was clearly reflected in their works.

Madonna of Loreto and Pilgrims by Caravaggio is now in Basilica di Sant Agostino.

Work on realism

The movement started with the work of the French author Stendhal. Honore de Balzac was seen as the father of realism with his Le Comédie Humaine, a multi-volumed interlinked collection of novels. This was followed by Gustave Flaubert's novel, *Madame Bovary*, which reflected Bourgeois ambience of its times. Guy de Maupassant, Joris Karl Huysmans, George Eliot, Thomas Hardy and Henry James were other authors whose works represented realism.

Realism in the ages

Realism, in a way, is about seeing things as they are, with little or no use of one's imagination. Realism, as an approach, can be found in Hellenistic structures, which accurately depicted certain elements of normal life. Caravaggio, Francisco de Zurbaran and Jose de Ribera were painters who were influenced by the Realism Movement.

Gustave Courbet, a French painter of the Realism Movement, opposed the academic neoclassical ideals and used mythological subjects.

Realism in literature

English writers like Daniel Defoe and Henry Fielding are great examples of authors who wrote on realistic themes. Balzac was another such writer who was influenced by the Realism Movement. In the book, *Le Comédie Humaine* or *The Human Comedy*, he spoke of real French problems like money, power, social status, patriarchy and matriarchy. Gustave Flaubert was another proponent of the realistic movement. His book, *Madame Bovary* was in fact an incisive account of the mentality of the French people.

A USSR postcard showing a painting by Jose de Ribera.

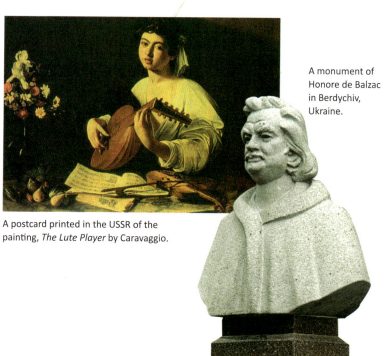

A postcard printed in the USSR of the painting, *The Lute Player* by Caravaggio.

A monument of Honore de Balzac in Berdychiv, Ukraine.

Scientific Positivism

The term "positivism" is all about a focus on positive sciences. It is something that can be tested and experienced. Auguste Comte was seen as the key supporter of positivism and he divided human history into three levels—religious, metaphysical and scientific. He stated that for the first two levels, humans tried to understand and explain things using personal feelings. In the third level, they focussed on observing and experimenting. These levels added to the development of humankind.

A monument of Auguste Comte, a French philosopher.

Emergence of sociology

In 1838, Comte came up with the term, "sociology". He used this term to describe a new way of looking at the society and promoted it as a different branch of study. His three-stage model of human knowledge explained the phases of religious and metaphysical world views that preceded the scientific approach to knowledge. His model also linked the data that he accumulated to form his theories.

New scientific foundation

Comte felt that everything from law to politics and religion should be rebuilt with a view of the newly formed scientific foundation. For example, according to Comte, religion needed to be about humanity and reason. It needed to have customs and symbols that were based on the new way

of thinking. Herbert Spencer and Thomas Huxley not only agreed with his thought but also propagated and studied sociology.

Twentieth century positivism

During the twentieth century, positivism gained a new avatar. It was known as logical positivism so that people do not confuse it with philosophy and its branches of study. It was also known as logical empiricism. It held that rationalism within the modern viewpoint was important. There are temples in Rio de Janeiro, Porto Alegre and Curitiba in Brazil and Paris that were built by nineteenth century Comtean positivists. In fact, even today London has a society of positivists.

Cesare Lombroso, an Italian psychiatrist and criminologist, was one of Comte's major supporters. Paul-Emile Littre and Louis Weber also studied from his ideas. John Stuart Mill would disagree with some points put forth by Comte, but also would agree with most. He wrote *System of Logic* in 1843, which expanded upon subjects like positivism, scientific reasoning and considered logic and mathematics to be empirical sciences. Herbert Spencer was considered second to him.

Thomas Huxley

Logical Positivism

Logical positivism was a movement which started in Vienna, Austria in the 1920s. People by now had started to focus on the scientific reasoning behind certain occurrences in nature. Also, scientific knowledge became popular because of its factual approach. A.J. Ayer's work first popularised logical positivism. It became extremely significant in the philosophy of science, logic and language. The movement believed that philosophy must avoid dogmatism, as done by science.

Statue of Sir Karl Popper at Vienna University.

Characteristics of logical positivism

Logical positivism is also referred to as "logical empiricism". It believed in rejecting metaphysical doctrines for their meaninglessness. It also promoted the opinion that the only factual knowledge is scientific knowledge. Unlike the previous movements of a similar nature, which believed that one could gain knowledge by personal experience only, logical positivism believed that knowledge comes from experiments, verifications and attempts to confirm an idea. It does not believe that metaphysical doctrines are false, saying that there is some credibility to them. However, it believes that they are without meaning. It believed that questions about God and freedom cannot be answered as they are not meaningful questions.

mathematicians who would discuss common subjects before World War I. The group was displeased by the explanations provided about subjects like logical truths and natural sciences. Hans Hahn, a leader of the Vienna Circle, first presented his work *Logisch-philosophische Abhandlung*, in 1921 before his students of the University of Vienna. Positivism, an idea propagated by this movement, believes that knowledge on any subject is a positive data of experience and that a fact should be based purely on logic and mathematics. This train of thought was proposed by the Scottish thinker, David Hume in the eighteenth century. However, he classified this view under formal sciences.

Vienna Circle

The Vienna Circle is a group that founded logical positivism. It first came into action in 1929. It consisted mainly of physicists and

FAST FACT

A. J. Ayer's views shocked and upset those who followed metaphysical and aesthetic philosophies. They refused to take him seriously and considered his views as an expression of his tastes.

Statue of David Hume.